FISHERMAN
BIBLE STUDYGUIDES

Romans
The Christian Story

JAMES REAPSOME

D1512098

SHAW BOOKS
an imprint of WATERBROOK PRESS

Romans

A Shaw Book

Published by WaterBrook Press

2375 Telstar Drive, Suite 160

Colorado Springs, Colorado 80920

A division of Random House, Inc.

ISBN 0-87788-734-9

Printed in the United States of America
2003

10 9 8 7 6 5 4

Contents

How to Use This Studyguide

*F*isherman studyguides are based on the inductive approach to Bible study. Inductive study is discovery study; we discover what the Bible says as we ask questions about its content and search for answers. This is quite different from the process in which a teacher *tells* a group *about* the Bible—what it means and what to do about it. In inductive study God speaks directly to each of us through his Word.

A group functions best when a leader keeps the discussion on target, but the leader is neither the teacher nor the "answer person." A leader's responsibility is to *ask*—not *tell*. The answers come from the text itself as group members examine, discuss, and think together about the passage.

There are four kinds of questions in each study. The first is an *approach question*. Asked and answered before the Bible passage is read, this question breaks the ice and helps you start thinking about the topic of the Bible study. It begins to reveal where thoughts and feelings need to be transformed by Scripture.

Some of the early questions in each study are *observation questions*—who, what, where, when, and how—designed to help you learn some basic facts about the passage of Scripture.

Once you know what the Bible says, you then need to ask, *What does it mean?* These *interpretation questions* help you to discover the writer's basic message.

Next come *application questions,* which ask, *What does it mean to me?* They challenge you to live out the Scripture's life-transforming message.

Fisherman studyguides provide spaces between questions for jotting down responses as well as any related questions you would like to raise in the group. Each group member should have a copy of the studyguide and may take a turn in leading the group.

A group should use any accurate, modern translation of the Bible such as the *New International Version,* the *New American Standard Bible,* the *New Revised Standard Version,* the *New Jerusalem Bible,* or the *Good News Bible.* (Other translations or paraphrases of the Bible may be referred to when additional help is needed.) Bible commentaries should not be brought to a Bible study because they tend to dampen discussion and keep people from thinking for themselves.

SUGGESTIONS FOR GROUP LEADERS

1. Thoroughly read and study the Bible passage before the meeting. Get a firm grasp on its themes and begin applying its teachings for yourself. Pray that the Holy Spirit will "guide you into all truth" (John 16:13) so that your leadership will guide others.

2. If any of the studyguide's questions seem ambiguous or unnatural to you, rephrase them, feeling free to add others that seem necessary to bring out the meaning of a verse.

3. Begin (and end) the study promptly. Start by asking someone to pray that every participant will both understand the passage and be open to its transforming power. Remember, the Holy Spirit is the teacher, not you!

4. Ask for volunteers to read the passages aloud.

5. As you ask the studyguide's questions in sequence, encourage everyone to participate in the discussion. If some are silent, try gently suggesting, "Let's have an answer from someone who hasn't spoken up yet."

6. If a question comes up that you can't answer, don't be afraid to admit that you're baffled. Assign the topic as a research project for someone to report on next week, or say, "I'll do some studying and let you know what I find out."

7. Keep the discussion moving, but be sure it stays focused. Though a certain number of tangents are inevitable, you'll want to quickly bring the discussion back to the topic at hand. Also, learn to pace the discussion so that you finish the lesson in the time allotted.

8. Don't be afraid of silences; some questions take time to answer, and some people need time to gather courage to speak. If silence persists, rephrase your question, but resist the temptation to answer it yourself.

9. If someone comes up with an answer that is clearly illogical or unbiblical, ask for further clarification: "What verse suggests that to you?"

10. Discourage overuse of cross references. Learn all you can from the passage at hand, while selectively incorporating a few important references suggested in the studyguide.

11. Some questions are marked with a ✍. This indicates that further information is available in the Leader's Notes at the back of the guide.

12. For further information on getting a new Bible study group started and keeping it functioning effectively, read *You Can Start a Bible Study Group* by Gladys Hunt and *Pilgrims in Progress: Growing Through Groups* by Jim and Carol Plueddemann. (Both books are available from Shaw Books.)

Suggestions for Group Members

1. Learn and apply the following ground rules for effective Bible study. (If new members join the group later, review these guidelines with the whole group.)

2. Remember that your goal is to learn all that you can *from the Bible passage being studied.* Let it speak for itself without using Bible commentaries or other Bible passages. There is more than enough in each assigned passage to keep your group productively occupied for one session. Sticking to the passage saves the group from insecurity ("I don't have the right reference books—or the time to read anything else.") and confusion ("Where did that come from? I thought we were studying _____.").

3. Avoid the temptation to bring up those fascinating tangents that don't really grow out of the passage you are discussing. If the topic is of common interest, you can bring it up later in informal conversation after the study. Meanwhile, help one another stick to the subject.

4. Encourage one another to participate. People remember best what they discover and verbalize for

themselves. Some people are naturally shy, while others may be afraid of making a mistake. If your discussion is free and friendly and you show real interest in what group members think and feel, the quieter ones will be more likely to speak up. Remember, the more people involved in a discussion, the richer it will be.

5. Guard yourself from answering too many questions or talking too much. Give others a chance to share their ideas. If you are one who participates easily, discipline yourself by counting to ten before you open your mouth.

6. Make personal, honest applications and commit yourself to letting God's Word change you.

Introduction

*P*aul, the author of Romans, ranks with the great world-changers of all time. Having encountered Jesus Christ in a vision while en route to arrest Christians, he gave himself to Christ's purpose for his life: announcing the gospel to the Gentile world. Paul completed that mission. But Paul was much more than an itinerant evangelist and church planter; he was an intellectual giant. He had received the finest education of his time. He was zealous, uncompromising, courageous, and indefatigable. He endured illness, shipwreck, and imprisonment. He was also compassionate, seeing himself as a nurse bringing up newborn babies in the Christian faith.

Romans is the foundational document of Paul's entire system of theology. Its impact and influence in history have been immeasurable, inspiring such great men as Augustine, Luther, Bunyan, and Wesley. Through such individuals, Romans has shaped not only the history of the church but of the world.

At the same time, this letter is the keystone of faith and life for countless thousands of individuals today. We study it not only because it has influenced the past, but because it can change our own lives as well. It is the Christian's story.

We don't need to feel intimidated by the fact that Romans is a theological letter. Instead we should appreciate it for that very reason, since the validity of our own spiritual experiences must always be checked against theological truth in Scripture. Actually, we can never legitimately divide theology and practice. Paul binds them inseparably in this letter. After he drills theology into the minds and hearts of his readers, he calls them to transformed living.

So, we will study justification, reconciliation, righteousness, sin, and redemption, but we will also study how to be holy in daily conduct, how to live under government, and how to get along with fellow believers in the church and unbelieving neighbors across the street. Understanding the theology of Romans will pay rich rewards in knowing how to live a distinctively Christian life.

WHY WE NEED SALVATION

ROMANS 1

*T*here are two great spiritual realities: God's salvation and God's wrath. Both stem from his righteousness. In the opening chapter of his letter, Paul introduces himself and his mission. The doctrine of salvation—the good news of God's gift in Christ—occupies center stage. Paul looks at society and gives convincing evidence of humankind's sin and the need for salvation.

1. In popular thought, what reasons are commonly given for social and personal problems?

READ ROMANS 1:1-7.

2. From this preface what impression do you get of Paul?

of the gospel?

of Jesus?

of believers in Rome?

3. What was Paul's overriding purpose in life? Why?

4. Why is it important to know who you are and what you're living for?

5. If you could write an introduction of yourself like this one, what would you say about your relationship to Jesus?

to the gospel?

to other people in the world?

to fellow Christians?

READ ROMANS 1:8-17.

6. As Paul contemplated coming to Rome, what two major goals did he have in mind (verses 11-13)? How would he reach those goals (verse 15)? What words did Paul use to convey the intensity of his feelings about reaching these goals (verses 9-11,14,16)?

7. How did Paul see himself in relation to the Christians in Rome (verses 8-12)? Why would he have needed their encouragement? Why would Paul have been under obligation to the unbelievers in Rome (verses 13-15)?

⤹ 8. What was Paul's view of the gospel (verses 16-17)? Why might he have been tempted to be ashamed of it? Why wasn't he?

9. In what ways have you experienced God's power in the gospel in your life? What do you hope to contribute to and receive from fellow Christians? How can you fulfill your obligation to those who haven't yet received God's power in the gospel?

READ ROMANS 1:18-32.

10. Identify the specific sins for which people are accountable to God. Why do you think that, from God's viewpoint, such things as gossip and boasting are on par with murder (verses 29-30)?

11. Three times Paul said, "God gave them over" (verses 24,26,28). In each case, what did people do to warrant this action on God's part? What does this passage teach us about the root cause of sinful acts?

⤴ 12. What part of God's nature is highlighted by contrast with humankind's intellectual and moral decay? Is God's response reasonable? Why or why not?

13. If you are still on the way to accepting God's salvation, what steps can you take to continue your spiritual search? What truth about God and about yourself did Paul say you need to acknowledge? If you agree with Paul's diagnosis, what remedy have you found for yourself in Romans 1?

JUDGMENT FOR JEWS, TOO

ROMANS 2

fter looking at society in general, Paul focused on his own people, the Jews, and found them equally guilty before God. It is painfully difficult for religious people to admit their shortcomings, but, as Paul said, their profession makes them susceptible to hypocrisy. One's advantages can be one's downfall.

1. Why do you think modern people find the idea of judgment repugnant?

READ ROMANS 2:1-16.

2. What facts about God's judgment can you find in verses 1-11? What is the dangerous presumption Paul warned against in verse 4? What is the root

cause of a person's "storing up wrath" for himself or herself (verse 5)? What is the only way to escape God's wrath (verse 4)?

✎ 3. What two options for our future are described in verses 6-11. What determines which kind of future a person will experience?

Note: Doing good must be understood in the context of salvation by faith alone (Romans 1:16-17; 3:21-24; 5:1).

✎ 4. Rome had a mixed population of Jews—those having the written laws of Moses in the Old Testament—and Gentiles who had no such written revelation—those without the Law. Why will both Jews and Gentiles deserve God's judgment (verses 12-14)? In addition to lawbreaking, what else will God judge (verses 15-16)?

5. How does the bad news of impending judgment prepare a person to believe and act on the good news of the gospel: that Jesus died to take away the judgment that each of us deserves? In a conversation with a friend who seems concerned about his or her fate, how would you summarize the main facts of this passage in your own words?

Read Romans 2:17-29.

6. In verses 17-20, Paul described, hypothetically, a very religious person. What inner qualities does his person have? What religious works does he or she do? In spite of good works, of what major sin is this same person guilty (verses 21-24)? Does this description fit you or anyone you know?

7. When a Jew sinned in this historical setting, what happened to God's name as a consequence (verse 24)? How should this fact influence your behavior?

Note: Circumcision (verses 25-29) was the physical sign of the Jews' covenant with God. (See Genesis 17.)

⌀ 8.   What were some of the Jews doing that resulted in their nullifying the value of their covenant? In addition to an outward sign of circumcision, what else does God look for (verses 28-29)?

9.   If having the Law (verses 17-24) and being circumcised (verses 25-29) could not achieve salvation, what can? How do you know?

10.   Are you trusting in some religious rite you experienced years ago? What evidence of "heart circumcision" do you see in your life?

DIAGNOSIS AND CURE

ROMANS 3

*P*aul develops the salvation theme by presenting the doctrine of justification—how a person with faith in Christ is given right standing before God. God justifies the penitent sinner on the basis of faith alone, not by virtue of any good works.

1. Why do people resist the idea that they need God's salvation?

READ ROMANS 3:1-8.

2. With what were the Jews entrusted (verse 2)? What was their responsibility in light of this calling? For what are you accountable before God?

3. How were some of the people trying to justify their sin (verses 5-8)? In what ways do people try to justify their sin today?

⌀ 4. Which of God's attributes did Paul defend? Why?

5. What role does admitting your just condemnation before God play in finding salvation in Christ? How does receiving Jesus as Lord and Savior uphold both the faithfulness and justice of God?

READ ROMANS 3:9-20.

6. What main point about humankind did Paul prove
   by his lengthy quotation from the Psalms and Isaiah
   (verses 10-18)? What is your response to this indict-
   ment? Why?

7. If you were writing a concise description of the
   problems of human beings, what conditions would
   you include? Would you include verse 18? Why or
   why not?

8. Who holds all of us accountable for our deeds
   (verse 19)? Why is it impossible to stand perfect
   before God on the basis of a religious code (verse 20)?

9. Paul used Scripture authoritatively to support his diagnosis of the human condition. What role does Scripture play in helping you understand and evaluate yourself? What steps can you take to develop a more disciplined approach to handling Scripture?

READ ROMANS 3:21-31.

10. In what ways has the righteousness of God been made known (verses 21-22)?

11. How are people justified (given right standing, declared righteous) before God (verse 24)? Why does everyone need to be justified (verse 23)?

12. What is our part in being justified (verse 26)? What was Jesus' part in justifying us (verses 24-25)?

13. Do our best efforts to earn righteousness before God really count for anything? Why or why not?

14. On what basis are both those who observe religious laws (Jews) and those who don't (Gentiles or "uncircumcised") justified?

15. Restate the main point of this section in your own words. Pretend you are explaining it first to a Jewish friend, then to a Gentile friend. What would you say in each case? Why?

RIGHTEOUSNESS BY FAITH

ROMANS 4

*A*braham looms large on the stage of salvation history. His faith relationship to God is at the heart of this chapter. In Christian doctrine, those who follow his example of faith are called Abraham's children.

1. What are some examples of human achievement that people are counting on to earn God's favor?

READ ROMANS 4:1-12.

2. On what basis was Abraham given righteousness (justification) before God (verses 3,9,11,22)? From a

human standpoint, what could the founder of the
Jewish nation have had to boast about before God?
Which of your own "works" commend you to God?

3. Describe the kind of people God justifies (verse 5)
    and blesses (verses 7-8). What is the wrong way to
    go about achieving righteousness? the right way?

⚘ 4. What argument did Paul use to show that the gift
    of righteousness by faith (justification) is available
    to all people, not just the physical descendants of
    Abraham (verses 9-12)?

READ ROMANS 4:13-25.

5. What promise did God give to Abraham (verses
    13,17-18)? What could have made it hard for
    Abraham to believe (verse 19)?

6. On what did God's promise rest (verse 16)? What
    was Abraham's part (verses 16,18-22)?

7. What did Abraham gain in addition to physical
    descendants (verse 22)? How do we receive right-
    eousness from God (verse 24)? On what facts about
    Jesus does our righteousness rest (verse 25)?

8. Meditate on Abraham's struggle to believe God's
    promise (see Genesis 15:1-3; 16:1-4; 17:1-2,15-18;
    18:10-12; 21:1-6). Do you find it hard to believe God's
    promise to give you his righteousness solely on the
    basis of your faith? Why or why not? If you do, what
    would it take to fully convince you that God will do
    what he has promised (verse 21)?

PEACE WITH GOD

ROMANS 5

What are the practical outcomes of faith in Christ? Having peace with God transforms everyday experience—even suffering. This chapter helps us to appreciate the new way of life compared to the old.

1. How does God's grace make a difference in the experiences of your everyday life?

READ ROMANS 5:1-11.

2. Describe those who have been justified by faith (verses 1-5). What do they have? What do they rejoice in? Why?

Note: To "have peace with God" (verse 1) means to be reconciled to him. In addition to justification and righteousness, reconciliation is another one of Paul's favorite pictures of the Christian's standing with God.

3. What is your attitude toward suffering? How does the outpouring of God's love help the believer respond positively to suffering (verse 5)?

4. List the different words used in verses 6-11 to describe humankind's basic spiritual condition toward God. What did it cost the Lord Jesus to correct this condition and make peace with God possible (verse 11)?

5. After you have settled a difference or a dispute with someone, how do you feel? Why? God has offered peace to his enemies. Why don't they accept it? What can you do to help them?

READ ROMANS 5:12-21.

6. What did Adam bring into the world? With what disastrous consequences?

7. What did Jesus give to the world? With what benefits?

8. How do you use the word *grace* in everyday life? What is the definition of God's grace according to this passage? Why is grace hard to accept?

9. Summarize this passage by listing everything you
    can find about Adam and Christ. Compare and
    contrast your lists.
    Adam

    Christ

10. Have you confessed your identity with Adam? with
    Christ? Why or why not?

ALIVE IN CHRIST

ROMANS 6

*C*hapter 6 of Romans is the key to overcoming sin's power. It is the cornerstone of Christian character. Paul's teaching about salvation now extends to right living. Jesus died to make us good in God's sight.

1. What kind of self-help schemes have you encountered that promise to make you a better, more successful person?

READ ROMANS 6:1-11.

2. In this passage Paul challenges one way of viewing ongoing sin. Describe this attitude. When, if ever,

have you reacted like this? How would such an attitude on your part trivialize or cheapen God's grace?

3. What was Paul's response to this attitude? What fact did he cite to prove his case?

4. With what events in Christ's life is the believer identified? With what consequences?

✐ 5. Describe in your own words what the following phrases mean in your everyday Christian experience: "dead to sin but alive to God" (verse 11); "old self was crucified…no longer be slaves to sin" (verse 6).

6. As you reflect on your constitutional freedom from sin through faith in Christ—your spiritual "Bill of Rights"—how would you evaluate your life?

7. What practical encouragement do these verses give you in your battle with sin?

READ ROMANS 6:12-23.

✐ 8. What practical commands did Paul give in verses 12-13? In what facts are these commands rooted?

9. What practical risk arises from living under God's grace (verse 15)? What did Paul say about this possibility?

10. What two kinds of slavery did Paul identify? What does each one lead to?

✐ 11. To what kind of slavery is the Christian committed? On what basis? With what consequent responsibilities?

12. Note the contrasts between those who have not yet accepted the gift of eternal life in Christ and those who have (verses 20-23). What differences do you see between these two groups of people? In which camp are you? How do you know?

STRUGGLING WITH SIN

ROMANS 7

S truggle against the oppression of sin's power is part of every Christian's life. Paul described his own battle with sin in chapter 7. This graphic picture helps us to know the enemy's power and how to overcome it.

1. Think of people you interact with every day. Is victory over sin a compelling issue with them? Why or why not?

READ ROMANS 7:1-6.

 2. To what subject does Paul now turn? Why? What did "the law" mean to his Jewish readers? What would be a parallel in your life?

Note: "The law" referred to in this passage is specifically that of Moses, found in Exodus through Deuteronomy.

3. "Brothers" refers to Paul's fellow believers in Christ. What facts did he tell them about themselves (verses 1,4)? On what basis could he pronounce them dead to and free from the Law?

4. How does the illustration of the husband's death support Paul's main point?

5. Compare the spiritual realities of the two main conditions Paul described in verses 5-6. Put the practical differences in your own words.

⌀ 6. The hypothetical wife described in verses 1-3 is free to remarry. Following the marriage analogy, what does it mean to you to "belong to another" (i.e., to Jesus) and to "bear fruit to God"?

READ ROMANS 7:7-13.

7. What question did Paul raise in this passage? What was his response?

⌀ 8. What was the purpose of the Law? What evidence of the working out of this purpose did Paul see in his life?

9. List all the facts about sin you can find in this passage. Summarize Paul's main point in your own words.

10. Paul's definition of and reaction to sin is highly personal. In what ways have you acknowledged sin to be the deadly enemy it is? Based on your study of Romans thus far, why is it essential to look at sin this way?

READ ROMANS 7:14-25.

11. What word did Paul use to describe the Law in verse 14? to describe himself?

What personal experience did Paul refer to as proof of his conclusion about himself (verses 15-20)? To what did he attribute his failure to do the right and the good?

12. Is Paul's experience of moral failure unique to him, or is it universal? Explain your response. In what ways has your experience matched his?

13. What further description of himself does Paul give in verses 23-24? What is the cause of his condition (verses 21-23,25)? How does this explain his conclusion at the end of verse 18?

14. Who has the answer to Paul's dilemma (verse 25)?
    How does what you learned in Romans 3–6 support
    Paul's conclusion in this passage? In what ways have
    you been freed from your failure to live up to your
    own moral code?

STUDY 8

THE FINISH LINE

ROMANS 8

*L*ike a weary marathon runner nearing his goal, Paul turns the corner in chapter 8 and triumphantly races for home—the certainty of God's presence and protection. No doubts assailed him now. Here is the finish line for those who trust in Christ.

1. What would you identify as the chief causes of mental and emotional distress today?

READ ROMANS 8:1-8.

2. What great foundational fact is true of those who believe in Jesus (verse 1)? To what were we

condemned? On what basis are we spared this judgment (verse 3)?

3. Compare "sinful nature" ("flesh," RSV) and "Spirit" as alternative ways of life. What are the eternal consequences of each? What evidence of each do you see at work in your life?

4. Some people are "in Christ Jesus" (verse 1) and some are controlled "by the sinful nature" (verse 8). From what you have observed in Romans thus far, how does one make sure he or she is "in Christ Jesus"? Support your answer with specific verses.

Read Romans 8:9-17.

5. List the "if" clauses in verses 9-11 (e.g., "if the Spirit of God lives in you"). State what is true for the one who meets each condition. Have you met the conditions, or are you still on the way? How do you know?

6. What is the binding obligation upon those in whom Christ and the Holy Spirit are living (verses 12-13)? What is promised to those who live up to that obligation? to those who don't?

7. What exalted positions and privileges are held by those who belong to Christ and are led by the Holy Spirit (verses 14-17)? What is the condition for sharing in Christ's glory (verse 17)? What do you think this means?

8. In what ways does your life reflect to others that you are God's child and a coheir with Christ? What changes would you like to see in your life that would make this reflection clearer? What can you do to start making these changes?

READ ROMANS 8:18-27.

9. What human problems did Paul address in verse 18? From what perspective does he view these problems?

10. According to verses 19-21, what is ahead for the created world? for believers in Christ (verses 22-23)? How can these promises help us cope with present suffering?

11. What is *hope* according to verses 19-20,24-25? Why is hope so important to a believer?

12. What is the Holy Spirit's ministry in relation to our suffering and weakness (verses 26-27)? In difficult times, what difference does prayer make—your own prayers and those of others for you?

READ ROMANS 8:28-39.

13. List everything God does for the believer in Christ (verses 28-30). What effect do these facts have on your perspective concerning your present circumstances and your future?

14. What is your answer to Paul's questions in verses 31-32? What is the basis of your answer?

15. What is the core question, stated somewhat differently, in verses 33-34? What was Paul's response? What facts did he cite as supporting evidence?

16. What kinds of experiences would cause a Christian to raise the question in verse 35? In what circumstances have you asked it? What was Paul's answer? How could he be so sure?

17. Review Romans 8 and list all the evidence for God's love for you in Christ. How strong is God's love for you? What needs in your life can God's love meet?

GOD'S SOVEREIGN CHOICE

ROMANS 9

*P*aul's anguish over Israel, as expressed in chapter 9, grows out of deep personal passion. How could all of God's blessings for Israel be in vain? For peace of mind, Paul rests in God's superior wisdom and knowledge.

1. In what circumstances do people feel cheated by God? Why?

READ ROMANS 9:1-5.

2. What feelings did Paul express in verse 2? What did he wish for himself? Why do you think his feelings were so intense?

✎ 3. List the advantages attributed to the Jews (verses 4-5). Summarize the significance of these advantages in terms of Israel's relation to God. What, in effect, canceled out these spiritual assets?

✎ 4. What evidence in the passage indicates that Paul considered the Jews to be in a perilous spiritual condition? Would you agree, considering what you have learned in Romans so far? Why? Cite scripture references in your response.

5. What does Paul's anguish over spiritual danger suggest about your attitude toward those who have yet to place their faith in Christ? What friends do you agonize over in prayer, and to whom do you show loving concern?

READ ROMANS 9:6-18.

✐ 6. Which of Abraham's sons was chosen to be the line
of his descendants? Who, therefore, was not chosen?

Note: "Natural children" (verse 8) refers to Ishmael and his descendants; "children of promise" refers to Isaac and his line.

✐ 7. What was unusual about God's choice of Jacob
instead of Esau? What reason did Paul give for
God's choice of Jacob? Was Jacob inherently any
better than Esau (verses 11,16)? What are the
implications of your answer?

8. What question did Paul raise in verse 14? In the story of Abraham, his children, and his grandchildren, why might someone consider God to be unfair? What was Paul's response?

Note on verses 12-13: As firstborn, Esau would have received a double inheritance. In this family the entire blessing of Abraham was involved (Genesis 28:4).

9. As you reflect on life, do you ever feel that God is unfair? In what circumstances? What comfort do you find in knowing that God is in control as opposed to chance or fate?

READ ROMANS 9:19-33.

10. How might some people respond to verse 18? Is this response appropriate? Why or why not (verses 20-21)?

✎ 11. According to verse 21, what two kinds of basic *human* pottery does God make? For what purposes (verses 22-23)? What is your answer to Paul's question in verse 21? in verses 22-24? Why?

12. What principle of God's sovereign choice of the people whom he has called to salvation is illustrated from Hosea and Isaiah (verses 24-29)?

13. What factor made the difference between the
    Gentiles who attained righteousness and the
    Israelites who didn't (verses 30-33)?

14. Is God obligated to save anyone? Why or why not?
    (Compare Romans 3:19,23; 6:23.) On God's part,
    what is required to save us (verses 15-16,24)? On
    our part, what must we avoid (verses 32-33)?

15. Why do you think God used the term "stumbling
    stone" to describe Jesus (verse 32)? Have you
    received God's mercy in Jesus Christ?

OBEDIENT PROCLAIMERS

ROMANS 10

*G*od's salvation works through human messengers. His plan is not thwarted by Israel's rejection. In chapter 10, Paul calls for obedient faith and for obedient proclaimers of Christ's message.

1. What influences in today's culture make it difficult for Christians to be Christ's messengers? Why is it difficult for people to hear and receive the good news of salvation?

READ ROMANS 10:1-13.

2. What was Paul's concern for his fellow Israelites (verse 1)? What major obstacle stood in their way (verses 2-4)?

3. Summarize what you have learned thus far in your study of Romans about the relationship between Christ, the Law, justification ("righteousness"), and faith (verse 4).

4. Read Deuteronomy 30:11-16 to get the context of verses 6-8. How did Paul apply this to Jesus and the gospel? What is Paul's main point? Why should it be easier to trust Jesus than to keep the Law?

5. Note Paul's emphasis on the word *saved* (verses 1, 9-10,13). According to Paul's writings to the Romans up to this point, what does it mean for a

person to be saved? From what is a person saved? To what purpose?

6. What other terms did Paul use that would parallel "saved"? Based on the facts in verses 9-13, what would you tell someone else about how to be saved?

READ ROMANS 10:14-21.

7. What four things must happen in the process that leads a person to saving faith (verses 14-15)? Who sends the preacher? What scope would you give to your definition of "preacher"? Why?

8. What is the focus of the preaching (verse 17)? Why? What essential facts about Christ have you

learned from Romans that would be included in
the message?

9. What is the difference between hearing the gospel
    and believing it (verse 16)? Did Israel receive ample
    proclamation of God's truth? What did the Israelites
    lack (verses 18-21)?

10. What did God do when Israel refused to believe
    (verses 19-20)? How does this Old Testament fact of
    history strengthen Paul's claim in verses 4,12-13?

11. As you reflect on the phrase "disobedient and obsti-
    nate people" (verse 21), what can you do to help
    Jewish friends to faith in Christ? In what ways can
    your feet be beautiful (verse 15)?

CHOSEN BY GRACE

ROMANS 11

ccording to chapter 11, God has not turned his back on Israel forever. Today, everyone and anyone can turn to Christ in faith. God's mercy extends to all. People may reject his mercy, but his grace will continue to work through others. He is the goal of all life, and he will receive the glory forever.

1. What things does God use to soften hard, unresponsive hearts?

READ ROMANS 11:1-12.

2. What fundamental question did Paul raise in verse 1? Why would this be a logical question to ask? What was Paul's answer? On the basis of what evidence (verses 1-5)?

⚙ 3. In verse 5, who does the chosen "remnant" refer to?
      What is the means of their salvation?

⚙ 4. How did Paul describe Israel's present spiritual con-
      dition (verses 7-10)? To whom did Paul attribute it?
      Is Israel therefore guiltless? Why or why not?

   5. What is the consequence of Israel's transgression
       (verses 11-12)? What hope did Paul hold out for
       Israel? In what sense have you received riches
       because of Israel's failure? What is your responsi-
       bility in light of this?

READ ROMANS 11:13-24.

   6. What ultimate destiny does Paul see for his fellow Jews (verses 14-16)? To whom does "holy dough" and "holy root" refer (verse 16)?

   7. To what are believing Gentiles compared (verse 17)? To what are unbelieving Jews compared (verses 17-19)? What is the relation of the "root" to the grafted wild olive tree? In what sense is this true?

   8. What is the basic difference between the broken branches and the grafted shoots (verse 20)? What warning did Paul give to the grafted shoots (verses 21-22)?

9. What hope did Paul hold out for the unbelieving branches (verses 23-24)? Look up the word *graft* in the dictionary. What facts from this analogy help you understand and appreciate your relationship to Jesus Christ?

READ ROMANS 11:25-36.

∂ 10. What is the "mystery" about Israel that Paul revealed in verses 25-27? Why did he explain it to the Gentiles at this time (verse 25)? How would the promise of Israel's future salvation prevent a Gentile from being conceited?

✒ 11. Who will be instrumental in bringing about Israel's salvation (verse 26)? What will he do? For whose sake is Israel beloved by God (verse 28)?

12. In verses 30-32, what one word—used four times—describes Jews and Gentiles? What one word did Paul use four times to describe God's character in relation to both Jews and Gentiles? How does the picture of God's plan for salvation of Jews and Gentiles alike stimulate both our praise and our intercession for others?

13. In what ways does the benediction in verses 33-36 serve as a fitting climax for everything you have learned about God in chapters 9–11?

LIVING SACRIFICES

ROMANS 12

Sacrifice is not a popular idea these days, but it is the key to a fruitful Christian life. In chapter 12, Paul says that God's salvation gift compels us to live sacrificial lives. By choosing not to live according to the demands of culture, Christians can find a wide variety of significant ways to minister to each other and to the world.

1. What adjectives best describe the church life you know? Are there any aspects of church life you would like to change? Why?

READ ROMANS 12:1-8.

2. What was Paul's appeal in verse 1? his command in verse 2? What reasons did Paul give for his appeal and his command? If you were to do what Paul said,

what qualities of character and practice would mark your life?

In what specific ways is God calling you to be a "living sacrifice" right now?

3. According to verses 3-8, what facts are true of every member of Christ's body? Therefore, what attitudes should each member hold toward himself or herself? toward each other?

4. List the gifts that have been given to believers (verses 6-8). Are any of these gifts more important or more

useful than the others? Why or why not? Why do you think Paul had to tell these Christians to use their gifts?

5. Two important considerations affect our success as members of Christ's body: function and relationship (verses 4-5). Why do we sometimes emphasize the one (i.e., doing church activities) and overlook the other (i.e., getting to know people, being open and honest, genuinely being part of a fellow member's life)? How can you keep these two areas in balance?

READ ROMANS 12:9-21.

6. Give specific examples of how one would obey Paul's commands in verse 9. Cite some cases of not obeying them.

7. According to verses 10 and 13, how should believers get along with each other? Give practical examples from everyday life.

8. What do the commands of verse 11 mean? How would you carry them out? Reflect on the implications of verse 12. How are you doing in these areas?

9. Toward whom does Paul direct Christian responsibility in verses 14-21? Why? Identify people you know who are representative of each group mentioned. What opportunities has God given you to bless, rejoice, and mourn?

10. Why is revenge so devastating to Christians (verses 17-19)? What does it require of your relationship with God not to take matters into your own hands?

SUBMISSION TO AUTHORITY

ROMANS 13

*G*od's salvation plan concerns secular society. In this chapter Paul addresses the Christian's response to civil authority. Whether we realize it or not, our conduct as Christians does make a difference. Faith in Christ compels us to accept God's standard of holiness.

1. What hard decisions do Christians living under oppressive governments have to make?

READ ROMANS 13:1-7.

2. What is the Christian's basic responsibility to his or her government? Why? What characterized the government to which Paul was subject at the time he

wrote this chapter? What light does this shed on
Paul's command?

3. According to verse 1, what is the origin of every
    government? What purpose is the government sup-
    posed to fulfill? What warnings did Paul give to
    those who would resist authority and refuse to be
    subject to the government?

4. In what sense is paying taxes a spiritual service?
    What instructions did Paul give concerning debt?
    Why might it be harder to show honor and respect
    than to pay taxes?

5. Give specific examples in your life of being subject
   to authorities, doing good, resisting government,
   doing wrong. What limits, if any, are there to a government's control over you? (Compare Acts 5:27-32
   with Matthew 22:15-22.)

READ ROMANS 13:8-14.

6. How did Paul summarize the Christian's social
   duties in verses 8-10? In what sense is this the fundamental ethic of all Scripture? (Compare Exodus
   20:13-17; Leviticus 19:18; Matthew 19:16-19;
   Mark 12:28-31.)

7. In what ways do you show love and care for yourself? How can you treat others with that same kind
   of love and concern?

✐ 8. In what specific areas of social conduct does Paul
appeal for reform (verse 13)? Why (verses 11-13)?

9. What two things are Christians told to put on or
arm themselves with (verses 12,14)? What does
"armor of light" suggest to you? Why?

10. How can you clothe yourself with Jesus (verse 14)?
In what ways does he help you withstand evil
desires?

A SPECIAL FAMILY

ROMANS 14

*G*od's people belong to a special family, the church. In chapter 14, the rules of family life are outlined. Not everyone in the family agreed, so Paul told them how to handle their differences. Mutual respect and love are expected of each member.

1. What characteristics tend to separate people? to draw them together? Why?

READ ROMANS 14:1-12.

2. What were the areas of contention in the church at Rome (verses 2-3,5-6)? What two basic commands did Paul give to resolve these issues (verses 1,3)?

3. Why is it wrong to look down on, condemn, or judge a brother or sister in Christ (verses 3-4,6, 10,12)? To whom do believers ultimately belong (verses 7-9)? Why? What effect does this fact have on your attitude toward fellow Christians?

4. Contrast the two judgments discussed by Paul: one believer judging another and God judging all believers (verses 10-12). What differences do you notice? How does the prospect of together facing a common judge deter criticism of one another?

5. What "disputable matters" divide believers today? Why? What can you do to prevent this disharmony and promote acceptance of each other in your family of believers?

Read Romans 14:13-23.

6. According to verse 13, what basic rule should guide
    us in promoting harmony in our Christian fellow-
    ship? As you reflect on the scene in the church at
    Rome described in this chapter, what things would
    be likely to cause a brother or sister to stumble?

7. How does Paul flesh out his teaching on the dangers
    of causing a brother or sister to stumble? Define
    it according to Paul's descriptions in verses 15-16,
    20,23. Why is causing someone to stumble such a
    serious offense?

8. What are higher priorities for Christians than eating
    and drinking (verses 17-19)?

9. What principle did Paul establish about the value of
    meat and drink itself (verses 14,20)? What deter-
    mines whether I myself should eat or drink
    (verses 21-23)?

10. Cultures change and differ from one another. Over
    what practices are Christians divided, and at times
    offended, in your particular culture?

11. Was Paul suggesting that my conduct should be
    determined by the fear of criticism from other
    Christians? Why or why not? What specifically
    would a critical brother or sister have to do before I
    would be guilty of causing him or her to stumble?

ONE HEART AND VOICE

ROMANS 15

fter summarizing the need for unity among Christians, Paul details in chapter 15 his own missionary purpose and vision. He was on the move for the sake of Jesus and the gospel. The apostle offered insights not only about his plans but also about his personal needs.

1. What marks those who have a passion for advancing the knowledge of Christ around the world?

READ ROMANS 15:1-13.

2. What principles did Paul give for building strong relationships in God's family (verses 1-2,7)? Who is our great example (verses 3,8)?

3. How did Jesus demonstrate the meaning of these principles? What did it cost him?

∂ 4. For what reasons did Jesus become a servant (verses 8-9)? Why did Paul cite so many Old Testament references concerning God's purpose for the Gentiles (verses 9-12)?

5. What attitudes did Paul stress as essential to living in harmony with one another (verses 4-5,13)? Why? What is the ultimate purpose for Christians getting along with each other (verse 6)?

6. As you reflect on your own relationships with fellow believers, how do Paul's prayers (verses 5-6,13) address your needs and interests? What are his two basic requests?

Read Romans 15:14-21.

7. How does Paul justify writing this letter (verses 14-16)? What did he understand his ministry to be?

8. On what basis could Paul be proud of his work (verses 17-21)? To whom did he give credit? Why? What did God accomplish through him? How?

9. What was the geographic extent of Paul's ministry? the spiritual extent? What was his overriding passion? Why?

10. In what ways could you make the focus of Paul's life your focus as well? your church's? What can you do to establish priorities for making Christ known where he is not known?

READ ROMANS 15:22-33.

✐ 11. What was Paul's ultimate destination (verse 24)? What was he anticipating from his stop at Rome (verses 24,32)? Why did Paul now feel free to visit Rome (verses 23-24)?

12. What was Paul's immediate destination (verse 25)? Why? What was his rationale for the offering from the Greek churches for the needy at Jerusalem (verses 26-27)? How is this principle carried out in your individual giving? in your church's giving?

13. What was Paul's special prayer request at this time (verses 30-33)? On what basis did he appeal to the believers in Rome?

14. Imagine that you are a Christian at Rome. How might you feel about Paul? about your part in his pioneering preaching? What could you possibly do to refresh him? How might your actions also refresh you?

LIFE TOGETHER IN CHRIST

ROMANS 16

*A*s we read the conclusion of Paul's letter, we are reminded of the value of deep Christian friendships. We learn who his partners in ministry were—twenty-two of them at least, including eight women. Their names also reveal the diversity among God's people, including Gentiles and Jews, slaves and freemen.

1. Of what value is it to be part of a church family consisting of people with different educational, economic, and social backgrounds?

READ ROMANS 16:1-16.

2. How did Paul describe Phoebe (verses 1-2)? What was his request on her behalf? Why?

3. Read Acts 18 for background on Priscilla and Aquila. For what did Paul commend them in verses 3-4? What was their role at Rome at this time (verse 5)? What would likely have been the characteristics of their service in a house church?

4. Identify the characteristics and qualities of the people to whom Paul sent greetings (verses 3-15). What traits stand out about these people? Would you feel at home among them? Why or why not? What would they contribute to your life? Explain your response.

5. Why do you think Paul went to the trouble to mention all these people by name? Why was such a network essential in the life of the early church? What does verse 16 reveal about life together in

Christ? What would be a modern counterpart of
the holy kiss?

6. What problem came to Paul's mind as he closed his
letter (verses 17-19)? What was the cause of the
problem? What was his solution?

7. What larger battle is being waged according to verse
20? What will be the ultimate outcome? How
would this knowledge encourage obedience? List
some ways you might obey the apostle's command
in verse 19.

8. What attributes of God do you find in Paul's benediction (verses 25-27)? Why are they appropriate to mention at this time? How can your worship of God be enhanced by thinking about what God is like?

9. What was the secret of strength for the Roman believers (verse 25)? What mystery has been revealed by God? For what purpose? What is the role of Jesus Christ in God's plan?

10. Write your own benediction in light of all you have learned in your study of Romans.

Leader's Notes

Study 1: Why We Need Salvation

Question 8. Chronologically, the gospel came to the Jews first (Acts 2:14-36), then to the Gentiles (Acts 10). Today, the gospel is freely available to all. There is no partiality with God. When Paul entered a city for the first time, he usually preached first in the Jewish synagogue.

Question 11. Paul was careful to show how God, as it were, allows sin to exact its horrible toll in human affairs. This principle is generally ignored when people look for the causes of social problems and human degradation. Man's willful rejection of God's rule and authority, in effect, turns him over to the rule of sin.

Question 12. It may be difficult to associate intellectual rebellion with moral decay because we generally hold a high view of human intellect. Also, modern man finds the wrath of God hard to accept. It sounds judgmental, unfair, and sub-Christian. Paul's argument is rooted in logic. Rationally, we accept the principle of punishment for lawlessness and wickedness.

Study 2: Judgment for Jews, Too

Question 3. Paul insisted that God is fair. His judgments are not based on how good we think we are. Truth and righteousness are the cornerstones of God's character. Therefore, Paul restated a universal principle: Those who do evil will be punished. In Romans 1:18–2:16, Paul made his basic case for God's justice in dealing with sin.

Question 4. Paul anticipated the "pleading of ignorance" of the Law as an excuse. He probed to the heart of the matter to show that inwardly we know the difference between right and wrong. There are no excuses for our sin before God.

Question 8. People usually flee to religious rites, traditions, and customs as a basis for hope and security. Paul showed that God's primary concern is the inner person, the condition of our hearts. Religion per se can keep us from knowing God.

Study 3: Diagnosis and Cure

Question 2. Paul affirmed a high view of the Old Testament revelation: "the very words of God" (Romans 3:2). This brought with it both responsibility and accountability for those who had received it.

Question 4. Focus on the character of God because one's faith and Christian growth must be rooted in who God is. Don't accept theological jargon. Be sure that the nature of God is defined in understandable terms. Use an English language dictionary.

Question 10. Ask for a variety of definitions of *righteousness* in this passage as compared to Romans 3:1-8.

Question 11. Look up the words *justified* and *justification* in a dictionary—both highly technical terms. Justification is the foundation of Paul's theological understanding. The future of one's Christian growth and assurance of salvation depends on a firm grasp of justification.

Question 13. This question highlights the crucial salvation issue for most people because most of us are firmly committed to the idea that we can somehow earn God's acceptance.

STUDY 4: RIGHTEOUSNESS BY FAITH

Question 2. Don't allow people to avoid this question. Give ample time for reflection. Encourage people to be honest. By this time, group members should feel safe enough with each other to explore this issue. In preparation, scan the heroics of Abraham in Genesis 12–25 to see what he could have boasted about.

Question 4. The rite of circumcision was a sign of the Jews' covenant relationship with God. Chronologically, Abraham was declared righteous before he was circumcised.

Question 7. The cornerstone of conversion is personal faith in Jesus Christ. Our faith rests in a historical person, not in vague theology. Allow people time to think about this foundational concept, which will be developed later on in Romans.

STUDY 5: PEACE WITH GOD

Question 8. Look up *grace* in a dictionary. Prepare some illustrations. Give the group ample time for reflection.

Study 6: Alive in Christ

Question 5. This is a very tough assignment. Be patient and allow for a variety of responses. Aim for clarity. Don't accept clichés. Prepare some illustrations. Be practical. Focus on the main principle: Death brings life and freedom. Just as we accept God's righteousness by faith, so we accept our death and self-crucifixion to sin by faith.

Question 8. "You are not under law, but under grace" (Romans 6:14). Christians do not live with an agreement of legal obedience to God, but with God's promise of forgiveness and justification as a free gift (grace) based upon their faith in Christ. The "thou shalt not" of the Law must give place to the power of the Holy Spirit. Paul developed this truth in Romans 7:1-6.

Question 11. Allow time to develop this concept in a variety of practical ways. Righteousness in this context means practical Christian living at every level: home, business, factory, school, church.

Study 7: Struggling with Sin

Question 2. After declaring the Christian's victory over sin (Romans 6:1-14), Paul used two illustrations: servant and master (6:15-18) and husband and wife (7:1-6). In effect, a new "husband" (Jesus) has replaced the Law. Christians are like a widow who has remarried.

Question 6. These spiritual abstractions must be fleshed out. Prepare specific examples of what they mean. Encourage the group to be practical. Think of several possible experiences to which these concepts might apply.

Question 8. "Once I was alive apart from law" (Romans 7:9) refers to a time when Paul lived free from any consciousness of sin. The phrase "sin, seizing the opportunity..." (verses 8,11) pictures sin working a strategy of conquest, using the Law as a base of operations.

Question 11. "The law is good" (Romans 7:16) in the sense that it condemns what Paul disliked. "It is no longer I myself who do it" (verse 17) did not relieve Paul of the responsibility for his sins. We are accountable for "sin living in" us. This fact gives rise to Paul's cry in verse 24.

Study 8: The Finish Line

Question 6. Give time for the group to develop what it means to "live according to the sinful nature" and to "put to death the misdeeds of the body." Aim for frankness and clarity. "Sinful nature" is the root of our sinful feelings and impulses. It expresses our pre-Christian way of life.

Study 9: God's Sovereign Choice

Question 3. "Adoption" here is national (Exodus 4:22), compared to personal (Romans 8:23). "Glory" refers to God's presence in the Shekinah cloud (Exodus 40:34-38). "Covenants" were never made with Gentile nations. The Law was not given to Gentiles. No promises have ever been given to a single Gentile nation.

Question 4. Prepare a brief summary of Paul's arguments about the Jews, going back to Romans 1. Ask different people to scan the chapter and summarize a paragraph or two.

Question 6. Verses 6-9 summarize Genesis 15–16; 18:1-15; 21:1-21; 24–25. Review these chapters for background information.

Question 7. God's choice, based on his mercy, is extremely difficult to comprehend from a human standpoint. Expect considerable discussion of this issue. Remember, there is no logical human explanation for it. It is a mystery of our faith that ultimately rests in the sovereign wisdom, love, and mercy of God. There's no need to try to defend it or God.

Question 11. This topic will generate considerable discussion. Encourage quiet, personal reflection and discourage acrimonious debate. Not everyone moves along at the same rate of spiritual comprehension. Allow "wrong" or partial answers to stand alone in the discussion. Your task is not to knock everyone into line, but to encourage the group to think, pray, and act according to Scripture.

Study 10: Obedient Proclaimers

Question 3. Don't skip summary questions. People need closure. You might ask someone to take each subject and prepare a brief summary. Remember to use your dictionary. Above all, aim for clear, specific, practical statements.

Question 4. "Verses 6-21 give an imaginary conversation between a Jew who says that he wants to be saved and a Christian Jew. *Jew:* 'Who will go up to heaven and bring down our Messiah?' *Christian:* 'He has come. He is Jesus.' *Jew:* 'But he died. Who will bring him up from the dead?' *Christian:* 'He has risen. If you will tell God that you believe that, sincerely, from your heart, you will be saved. God will save anybody who asks him to. You say that some cannot ask because they have never heard of him? It is not that they have not heard; everyone has heard of God (Romans 1:19-20), but they will not believe. And Israel has certainly heard of her Messiah, but has refused him, and God is saving Gentiles" (*Holy Bible, Pilgrim Edition,* Oxford University Press, pp. 1482-83).

Question 10. Try to place this ancient history in a variety of modern settings, both negative and positive. There are serious consequences to unbelief, but we cannot prejudge who might or might not be interested in hearing the gospel.

STUDY 11: CHOSEN BY GRACE

Question 3. Just as God preserved a "remnant" of 7,000 followers in the days of Elijah, so in Paul's time and ours there are a handful of Messianic Jews who firmly believe in Jesus as God's promised Messiah.

Question 4. "The picture of a blind, decrepit old man, bowed down in age and infirmity...is a very pathetic representation of a people in a state of religious senility" (E. K. Lee, quoted in *The International Bible Commentary,* edited by F. F Bruce, Grand Rapids, MI: Zondervan, 1986, p. 1337). The roots of anti-Semitism go deep among Christians. This scriptural teaching in Romans 11 does not warrant prejudice against Jews today.

Question 6. "The illustration of root and branches in verse 16 is developed into a horticultural allegory describing God's plan for present and future. The idea comes from Jeremiah 11:16 where Israel is compared with an olive tree, once having fruit beautiful in form, but now spoiled by sin and due for punishment: Its branches will be broken. Paul finds the current situation explained in this verse. The tree is the people of God. Its branches are living Jews. Now some of the branches, unbelieving Jews, have been pruned away and the only natural branches left are the believing remnant of Israel. But the divine Gardener has replenished the tree with a wild olive shoot.

"Gentile converts to Christianity comprise a cutting from an oleaster shrub inserted into the stock of the cultivated olive tree… But the Gardener has not finished his work yet. The natural branches that have been removed will one day be grafted in again, as soon as they cease to persist in unbelief. Now there are only a few Jewish branches left (cf. v. 17) in company with a large wild shoot taken from the Gentile world: They are all there because of their common faith, faith in God who has revealed himself through Jesus Christ. One day the Jewish and Gentile Christians will be joined on the tree by the mass of renegade Jews, who will come to share their faith and be restored as active members of the people of God" (*The International Bible Commentary,* p. 1337).

Question 10. "God's plan is in two stages. The first stage is the rejection of most of the Jews in order that God may make up the full number, which only he knows, of Gentile Christians. The second stage, which he will put into operation as soon as the first is completed, is a mystery, a secret design of God which human minds would not have hit upon apart from revelation. All Israel will be saved, brought into the Christian blessings into which now only a remnant of the Jews have entered. All Israel means the Jews as a collective whole, not the arithmetical sum of all individual Jews. The phrase is obviously contrasted with part of Israel, and Israel consistently refers to the Jews in chapters 9–11. *Saved is to be taken in the same spiritual sense as in verses 11,14"* (*The International Bible Commentary,* p. 1338).

Question 11. The Lord Jesus Christ is the promised deliverer (Isaiah 59:20-21), a picture alluded to by Paul in 1 Thessalonians 1:10, where Jesus "rescues us from the coming wrath."

STUDY 12: LIVING SACRIFICES

Question 2. Romans takes a very practical turn here, individually and corporately. Allow ample time to develop Paul's appeal and his command. Encourage specific examples from everyday life. These verses have often been the basis for a turning point in the lives of many Christians.

Question 9. It may take your group a while to focus specifically on groups or people. One reason is that some Christians have few, if any, close relationships with people outside the church. Encourage members to give specific examples and to admit their shortcomings if necessary.

STUDY 13: SUBMISSION TO AUTHORITY

Question 2. Read about the Roman Empire in an encyclopedia. Briefly summarize your findings.

Question 6. Emphasize the positive effects of Christian living. Don't take time to discuss all the commandments. Ask for recent practical demonstrations of love.

Question 8. "Salvation" in Romans 13:11 refers to the redemption of the body when it is either raised from the dead or caught up at Christ's return to meet him in the air (F. F. Bruce, *Romans,* p. 242).

Study 14: A Special Family

Question 4. "*Judgement Seat.* In Greek this is the word for the judges' stand at the Olympic races. Just as the Olympic contestants stood before the judges' stand to receive their laurels, so every Christian shall stand before Christ to receive any rewards he may have earned. Contestants should certainly not try to judge each other" (*Holy Bible, Pilgrim Edition,* p. 1487).

Question 7. Much confusion surrounds the concept of causing someone to stumble. Note that Paul's teaching goes much deeper than merely being criticized by a fellow Christian. Spiritual issues are at stake: Leading one's brother or sister into sin and destroying Christ's work in him or her.

Question 8. Take time for a thorough discussion of priorities and principles. This is foundational. Some members in your group may not have encountered these ideas before. Avoid debates about different values. Stick to biblical priorities in this passage.

Study 15: One Heart and Voice

Question 4. Keep in mind that the Jews held deeply ingrained prejudices against Gentiles, who were considered beyond all hope of God's grace and mercy. The Jews felt they had a corner on God's blessings.

Question 11. Paul wrote very honestly and personally here. Reflect on how this would have helped his readers. Note the universal scope of his mission.

Study 16: Life Together in Christ

Question 6. Here is another honest picture of church life. Sometimes we have such an exalted view of the early church that we overlook the problems, especially concerning people who exploited and divided the church from within.

What Should We Study Next?

*T*o help your group answer that question, we've listed the Fisherman studyguides by category so you can choose your next study.

TOPICAL STUDIES

Angels by Vinita Hampton Wright

Becoming Women of Purpose by Ruth Haley Barton

Building Your House on the Lord: Marriage and Parenthood
  by Steve and Dee Brestin

The Creative Heart of God: Living with Imagination
  by Ruth Goring

Discipleship: The Growing Christian's Lifestyle by James and
  Martha Reapsome

Doing Justice, Showing Mercy: Christian Actions in Today's
  World by Vinita Hampton Wright

Encouraging Others: Biblical Models for Caring by Lin
  Johnson

The End Times: Discovering What the Bible Says
  by E. Michael Rusten

Examining the Claims of Jesus by Dee Brestin

Friendship: Portraits in God's Family Album by Steve and
  Dee Brestin

The Fruit of the Spirit: Growing in Christian Character
  by Stuart Briscoe

Great Doctrines of the Bible by Stephen Board

Great Passages of the Bible by Carol Plueddemann

Great Prayers of the Bible by Carol Plueddemann

Growing Through Life's Challenges by James and Martha
  Reapsome

Guidance & God's Will by Tom and Joan Stark

Heart Renewal: Finding Spiritual Refreshment by Ruth
  Goring

Higher Ground: Steps Toward Christian Maturity by Steve
  and Dee Brestin

*Images of Redemption: God's Unfolding Plan Through the
  Bible* by Ruth Van Reken

Integrity: Character from the Inside Out by Ted Engstrom
  and Robert Larson

Lifestyle Priorities by John White

Marriage: Learning from Couples in Scripture by R. Paul
  and Gail Stevens

Miracles by Robbie Castleman

One Body, One Spirit: Building Relationships in the Church
  by Dale and Sandy Larsen

The Parables of Jesus by Gladys Hunt

Parenting with Purpose and Grace by Alice Fryling

Prayer: Discovering What the Bible Says by Timothy Jones
  and Jill Zook-Jones

The Prophets: God's Truth Tellers by Vinita Hampton
  Wright

Proverbs and Parables: God's Wisdom for Living by Dee
  Brestin

Satisfying Work: Christian Living from Nine to Five
  by R. Paul Stevens and Gerry Schoberg

Senior Saints: Growing Older in God's Family by James and
  Martha Reapsome

The Sermon on the Mount: The God Who Understands Me
    by Gladys Hunt
Spiritual Gifts by Karen Dockrey
Spiritual Hunger: Filling Your Deepest Longings by Jim and
    Carol Plueddemann
A Spiritual Legacy: Faith for the Next Generation by Chuck
    and Winnie Christensen
Spiritual Warfare by A. Scott Moreau
The Ten Commandments: God's Rules for Living by Stuart
    Briscoe
Ultimate Hope for Changing Times by Dale and Sandy
    Larsen
Who Is God? by David P. Seemuth
Who Is Jesus? In His Own Words by Ruth Van Reken
Who Is the Holy Spirit? by Barbara Knuckles and Ruth Van
    Reken
Wisdom for Today's Woman: Insights from Esther by Poppy
    Smith
Witnesses to All the World: God's Heart for the Nations
    by Jim and Carol Plueddemann
Women at Midlife: Embracing the Challenges by Jeanie
    Miley
Worship: Discovering What Scripture Says by Larry Sibley

BIBLE BOOK STUDIES

Genesis: Walking with God by Margaret Fromer and
    Sharrel Keyes
Exodus: God Our Deliverer by Dale and Sandy Larsen
Ezra and Nehemiah: A Time to Rebuild by James Reapsome

(For Esther, see Topical Studies, *Wisdom for Today's Woman*)

Job: Trusting Through Trials by Ron Klug

Psalms: A Guide to Prayer and Praise by Ron Klug

Proverbs: Wisdom That Works by Vinita Hampton Wright

Ecclesiastes: A Time for Everything by Stephen Board

Jeremiah: The Man and His Message by James Reapsome

Jonah, Habakkuk, and Malachi: Living Responsibly
    by Margaret Fromer and Sharrel Keyes

Matthew: People of the Kingdom by Larry Sibley

Mark: God in Action by Chuck and Winnie Christensen

Luke: Following Jesus by Sharrel Keyes

John: The Living Word by Whitney Kuniholm

Acts 1–12: God Moves in the Early Church by Chuck and
    Winnie Christensen

Acts 13–28, see *Paul* under Character Studies

Romans: The Christian Story by James Reapsome

1 Corinthians: Problems and Solutions in a Growing Church
    by Charles and Ann Hummel

Strengthened to Serve: 2 Corinthians by Jim and Carol
    Plueddemann

Galatians, Titus, and Philemon: Freedom in Christ
    by Whitney Kuniholm

Ephesians: Living in God's Household by Robert Baylis

Philippians: God's Guide to Joy by Ron Klug

Colossians: Focus on Christ by Luci Shaw

Letters to the Thessalonians by Margaret Fromer and Sharrel
    Keyes

Letters to Timothy: Discipleship in Action by Margaret
    Fromer and Sharrel Keyes

Hebrews: Foundations for Faith by Gladys Hunt

James: Faith in Action by Chuck and Winnie Christensen

1 and 2 Peter, Jude: Called for a Purpose by Steve and Dee
Brestin

How Should a Christian Live? 1, 2, and 3 John by Dee
Brestin

Revelation: The Lamb Who Is a Lion by Gladys Hunt

BIBLE CHARACTER STUDIES

Abraham: Model of Faith by James Reapsome

David: Man After God's Own Heart by Robbie Castleman

Elijah: Obedience in a Threatening World by Robbie
Castleman

Great People of the Bible by Carol Plueddemann

King David: Trusting God for a Lifetime by Robbie
Castleman

Men Like Us: Ordinary Men, Extraordinary God by Paul
Heidebrecht and Ted Scheuermann

Moses: Encountering God by Greg Asimakoupoulos

Paul: Thirteenth Apostle (Acts 13–28) by Chuck and
Winnie Christensen

Women Like Us: Wisdom for Today's Issues by Ruth Haley
Barton

Women Who Achieved for God by Winnie Christensen

Women Who Believed God by Winnie Christensen